Under Old Stars

★

Also by Chris Pannell

Fractures, Subluxations and Dislocations

Sorry I Spent Your Poem

Under Old Stars

Chris Pannell

Seraphim Editions

The publisher gratefully acknowledges the financial assistance of the Canada Council for the Arts.

Published in 2002 by
Seraphim Editions
970 Queen Street East
P.O. Box 98174
Toronto, Ontario
Canada M4M 1J0

The Canada Council | Le Conseil des Arts
for the Arts | du Canada

National Library of Canada Cataloguing in Publication Data

Pannell, Chris, 1956 –
        Under old stars

Poems.
ISBN 0-9689723-2-2

        I. Title.

PS8581.A64U64 2002   C811'.54   C2002-900467-5
PR9199.3.P36U64 2002

Editor: A.F. Moritz
Author and cover photo: Janice Jackson
Design: Perkolator {Kommunikation}

Printed and bound in Canada

Contents

Marking the Place with Ourselves

Years Later   9
Every Train and Station   10
Fire on Boxing Day   12
Poem of Gratitude, Exhaustion   13
On Blue Sheets   14
Topography   16
On the Dementia Ward   17
The Green Candy Dish   18
Rain at Cheticamp   19
Prayer for My Wife Learning to Drive ...   20
Two Kinds of Company   22
Monologue in a Furniture Shop   24
In Search of   25
The Man Who Grew Too Much   26
A Yard Sale   27

The Upward Climb

Rush Hour   31
The Silver Sky   34
At Durham Warehouse   36
Even When I Sleep, There's Paperwork   38
Click on OK   40
User Instructions   42
Insomnia   43
Sleep   44
Worry   46
Ice Overhead   48
Layoff Rumours   49
If Accountants Were Cowboys   50
Frank Is My Shepherd   51
Tremors   52

The Last Ride   *53*
Passing   *54*
Joe   *56*

Echoes of Wilderness
To Touch a Bird   *59*
Variation on Colville's *Hound in Field*   *60*
For the Mosquito   *61*
The Fin Whale at Cheticamp   *62*
Parrot Breeding Season   *64*
Trying to Mother   *66*
Lines Written after Watching a Huge Truck of
    Chickens Pass on the 401   *68*
Bird Watching   *70*
In Allan Gardens   *71*
More Rocky Mountain Views   *74*
Consumers   *76*
Muskoka Blues   *77*

Samizdat
Logos   *81*
Improvisation on a Hot Autumn Day   *82*
Poetry at the Jaffé Lounge   *84*
In the Bigger Bookstores   *86*
Tasnim Sings   *88*
Reverse Shoplifting   *89*
Variation on Beethoven's Violin Concerto   *90*

Marking the Place with Ourselves

And the angel,
when it comes, may not announce itself
with any buffeting of ears,
may not even whisper,
may not even be a full-fledged angel, may be
just an eddy of the air, which
catches the stuttered heart in its two-step
and is off.

– Hospital Zone
Don McKay

Years Later

I found
your photo
between the pages of a book
I lent you

That's where you stopped reading
and marked the place with yourself

Perhaps I lent this book to others
but their faces don't fly out when
I fan the pages
And you're stuck in that story
you didn't finish
troubled by something
Would you have asked me for help
if I'd noticed you waving
years ago?

Every Train and Station
for Moira Pannell

From your hospital bed you paraphrased
Oscar Wilde: *Either the beige goes or I do.*
I sat down, felt with my foot
your luggage, your fear stowed below.

I had come up the main walk from your future
through that old sixties space race architecture –
long boulevards, flying saucers on lamp posts,
abundant space for recovery.

And afterwards
under halogen lamp light
I waited on salt and asphalt for a train home
in an empty station that had been careless
with the commuters it held
but lost on rails too steel too cold.
In a black and white photograph
your four-year-old arms reach through the sleeves
of a white Sunday dress
and clutch a muddy soccer ball.

Our parents emigrated through
a small English station called Exodus
dreaming us among the other details –
a forest green with rain, steaming stony ground,
pale platform lights,
Moira don't lie down in these distractions.

Last night you woke, burning inside.
Tonight you look healthy, sleepy, cheeks red –
Get me up, you croak,
there's no dignity in a public bed.
OK, lie back while I, selfish to the end,
listen to you breathe,
a captive audience for my joking.
Your head tilts to me   and you sigh.

Fire on Boxing Day

A skyful of sparks flies into
the night, the bitter cold,
the house is surrendering,
the smell
　　　　of melted decoration in everybody's clothes.

Mars lights, red and orange, have intruded
under blinds, under our sleep
with ambulance and police cars.
A perfect fire set upon our neighbours' wooden deck,
they're trapped like an example in a book of why
we should take precautions.

In and out go fire fighters
to the sound of anonymous radio dispatch.
The pumper roars, they drag the pressure of the city
though the front door. Smoke thickens through
a hole in the roof with each blast of water.

At last the family appears from the stinking pyre,
safe, fuming – why me? And at Christmas time?
And I'll kill the bastard that did this,
and slippers and robe not right
for the asphalt drive covered with ice in the dark.
Each bystander in a parka shivers and
wonders why not me? and thank God,
though we all gave up believing in Him long ago.

So cold we clap our mitts
and watch His fallen angel
play with fire
dancing orange windy in the night.

Poem of Gratitude, Exhaustion

Hope is the whole contract,
the clauses you didn't read –
those not written, the book unfinished,
the child not conceived.

Up those stairs and down,
the cat in your arms grows lighter.
These are his last days, and still you think
perhaps the medication does some good.
Put him outside for fifteen minutes
to look at the old neighbourhood.

Any anniversary
represents the other 364 days
you have been at your life's work,
hemmed in with a jumpy heart.
The cat wants in, the cat wants out.
Service becomes its own reward –
the orange burning gleam
of the hardwood floor.

Our furry distraction flops in the sunlight
in the hall, panting, waiting.
No longer must we avoid his claws,
the tiger in his tabbiness
about to leap back into the wild.

On Blue Sheets

Rain has bounced on the road all day,
run down the windows of wards
where you work, where the elderly die.
After months of wavering,
their minds seep through the drugs,
dementia cracks and quashes all dams,
all sane efforts of family,
until at last, a sleeping death.

You speak
for their human needs and rarely raise
your voice but this morning
you snapped from the caseload and shouted at the nurses.
Apologized in the afternoon,
slammed our front door tonight,
burst out with the accusations
of family members who cannot cope with their father
losing the last of his marbles,
kicking other patients from his wheelchair.

After dinner and talk we can at last submerge
in bed. These storms will pass
though in your drowsy breath
I hear a tailwind. You slip asleep,
face in a frown, slow rippling lip,
and throw a cough past
my bedside umbrella of light.

I write another page,
expect you to wake and tell me *No*.
Hear the city hum with motor flow –
and I should stop, but the rain
has freed this night for us, like that
feather rising on the furnace heat.
The morning sun will catch you bright but
older, with five black hairs on your pillow.
I pray you will be praised.

Topography

She undresses
the lines on her skin make a relief map
of pressures

I move to touch the indentations
she starts
irritated
not used to being read

Faint shadows of roads
a blouse tucked under skirt all day
frills on flesh

She is tired, covers up with a housecoat
its grid of green plaid like a jail window

Bathwater, humidity
will erase those lines
and without direction
my fingers reach blind
across the unknown distance

On the Dementia Ward

Ghosts speak with the voice of Mr. Vukovar,
they howl and bay his rage,
then baby-like he groans
and sings the first line
of a nursery rhyme through a
wispy throat.

The flesh of his feet is barely contained
by pale skin, toenails
like bones tearing through
       threaten
this flimsy old world.
Somewhere down the long concrete hall
a toilet flushes incessantly.

And while I become angry with the plumbing,
I also see he has been swept away
by a force in the blood,
has been unleashed into scraping yelps,
he's probably savouring
that tang of urine in the air
that cannot be controlled by any cleaning,
his ghostly self
about to burst this technicality
of heartbeat and breathing.

The Green Candy Dish

A giant Christmas bauble squats
on the wood veneer,
the lid handle promises
after-dinner sweets. Get past
the green convex reflection where
faces slip aside and
all is belly.

Bend and stare at the mint surface,
see the possibility of chocolate,
sugar force against hunger
and the blues. Salivate
for a porcelain world so small, green,
appealing to tempted hands.

Freed from the dinner plate
we hover in a bloated state;
already trapped in the juices of digestion,
we reach for guilty inspiration.

Rain at Cheticamp

The minutes of a holiday
cannot tick away
          any more than
the melted clock in the Maritime Museum
showing 9:05 on the morning of the Halifax explosion.

The spent budget pauses
fiddles with pen and ledger
the family car has looked over
the parking situation, a lot
of asphalt and plans to walk the trails
washed and washed out again.
Even Cape Breton's drizzle takes its time
as do tales of maritime history –
how once the cod were so huge and thick
you could have walked their backs across the water
not quite like Jesus with his loaves and fishes
but somehow all this was meant to last forever.

Lobster Traps for Sale
stacked high on the roadside form a pyramid
of emptiness. Time slows
for the rock that resisted the last ice age.

And sure it's nice the youngsters
bypass the traditions of sea and catastrophe
but the way they're leaving now
empties every home and heart
just like that sea
and every logger every tree
has built hotels and here come those vacationers
in time for another storm.

Prayer for My Wife Learning to Drive a Car with Standard Transmission

not ready   ready
the car and she agree
I'm along for the ver ver ver ver vermilion
feeling in my heart and fingertips

morning sky clear
for lame instructions
I'd rather be in the wrong gear on the road
than the right gear in the ditch

let us intone the priorities
of live and let the other guy have the fast lane
perform the ritual of seatbelts and mirror adjustments
signifying the differences between bodies, perspectives

we've agreed to forestall
the moment when we must start
            on an incline
like childhood
                  the upward climb
always a damn new thing
three wiper speeds
night driving
to not panic over rain on a cloudless day

gently from the curb
first to second
in traffic it's easy to forget a gear
called reverse, to undo our mistakes
and back up through our relationship with

key   clutch   gas
tickturn
tickturn
indicator like a metronome

                    relaxes me
enough to stop hovering
over the hand brake to my left
and to enjoy her glide
into these nervy new powers

Two Kinds of Company

Her blue Japanese sports car
roars its perfect engineering
through winding country roads
and the Lincolnshire black night.
She has blonde shoulder-length curls.
She's neither too old
nor too young for me.

Past collapsing trees, foxes and bats that dart
too fast to really see
in the splattering rain,
her gear shifts up and down the scale,
her engine sings the lyric it knows,
through curves, down hills and valleys,
by hedges and stone walls.
We see only by headlights
and the car's console.
Somewhere behind must be the moon.

On the other side of Earth, you
are still in the sun. How warm, how it
lights the holes in my version of this story!
On we go through the dark
through her career as a dancer
and what audiences are like, and how her boyfriend
forgets her birthday.

And where exactly are you, beyond
the sea? At what street corner, at what table,
and what are you saying or hearing?
Like one of our green and noisy birds,
the last smile you gave me has leapt into the air
and flown the Westerlies. In an instant
it will descend, claws outstretched,
tear through this canvas top,
jump into my arms, a clutch of wild feathers.
It will grip my finger with its hard beak,
a more ferocious companion in the dark.

Monologue in a Furniture Shop

Along with a table and kitchen accessories,
pick out a cardboard TV,
a few shelves of phony books in leather bindings.
Each night the cleaners will dust
and remove the empty take-out boxes.
This might be the end of homelessness
as we've known it.

After hours it's quiet.
You'll get used to
the burgundy preferences of
stock brokers who can make things
rise and rise only. Let's shed our dishevelment
with a shower in the bathroom department.
Watch out for security. Hide anywhere.
Get into bed.

Tomorrow, if you're next to a customer,
          don't upset the sales force
by muttering. They might
see themselves, heads propped in hands
at this table, fighting off a terrible hunger,
their kids tied up in the armoire.

On the streets no one sees,
but in here, sound carries.
          Look, she's closing the sale,
I'll model and say nothing,
watch her fingers softly stroke
my pale leather couch.

In Search of

Trace of a cigar lingers in
halls and staircases
a musty shoe
the murderer's handgun
drawn curtains
the green-cut-grass odour of the gardener
the young boy's balsa-wood flyer

The novel stops at the moment of letting
page 267 and 268 touch again
so they cease to say what they know
about one thing leading to another

In my room, dusty white stipples hang down
from the ceiling above the corpse, myself
my eyes play out the adventure
recently bloodied with imagination
book plus me
and a non sequitur memory of
dust mites exploding from vacuum cleaner bags
violence begetting violence
magnifying glass held in the hot summer sun
trying to set the picnic table on fire
with boredom the world dies
smoke rises
the trouble, the story, the boy
and I
begin again

The Man Who Grew Too Much

Like a manic swelling superhero
you burst through the car's windshield at the moment
the expansive flat blue seemed
something to hold
beyond language, beyond sharing.

It was not enough that Earth had given food
and flesh of pleasure like warm water.
You grew as a mute giant.

Now you must be careful with such feet
not to destroy the surfaces on which you stand.
Everything has dwindled, your eyes so large and vision so poor.
You remember once looking up at skyscrapers,
churches without conscience.

This morning sky is as cool as your youth,
this Dominion of Canada so utterly dominated
you can throw the word aside,
hear it faintly crash into something.

Your arms embrace the thin mist,
your fingers poke holes in the clouds,
your elbows push the Gulf Stream.

You are the monument
before which birds die of fear.
Now is the time to embrace the sky,
its beautiful blue death,
leaving only dogs to eulogize.

A Yard Sale

so many
pink tiny toys
and children's clothes on the line
even out of doors the books are musty
the Philharmonia Orchestra
Otto Klemperer conducting
is warping in May sunshine
in the cardboard box
the unkept offered to another keeper
> *hey I'll pay them to take it away*
> *nickel, dime, gimmie a toon for that*

the broken laptop computer goes for a song
though it never knew any form of music
> *that tractor don't cut grass*

the sun rises over stuff
not quite beat enough
to throw away
the exercise bike that went nowhere
the wheelchair of a dead sister

at a yard sale
> anything will land
in a stranger's hand
a violin is playing Tchaikovsky
allegro moderato
> a folk tune from a gypsy dream has squealed its way
through Russia's Imperium
> into a Canadian day on Lake Simcoe
fifty cents, make me an offer

back home the record's cleaned
virtuosity gleams in a young girl's ears
her grandfather revisits Sunday evenings
at the Royal Albert Hall, his young lankiness crammed
into the poor seats up near the organ pipes
better to feel the heaven of rising things
she picks up his coin of memory
imagines a red velvet dress
fire-notes spitting from her shoulder

The Upward Climb

Then it was all over, the warring factions
were satisfied, the self-help manual
for the unemployed was finished and so was I.

– Artisan and Clerk
A.F. Moritz

Rush Hour

1.
i have all this time to study vinyl
rivets
shell pattern plastic
fern green footrests
rubber and chrome

i have an hour that lasts forever
time enough to scratch out a novel
reconcile East and West
raise a family

but the armrests on this seat don't flip up
like my erect imagination

2.

imagine the weary patience of my boss
lateness which is not a state of time but
his state of mind
picture an industrial film
robots move quickly back
                and forth
doing glamorous work for the advertisers
spot welding
assembling night and day

here six lanes of red and white lights
        stop and start
        cross the median
        into a grey horizon
        so much new and shiny metal
        drivers hunched over steering wheels
pinched lips hold in choice words
me fidgeting the adjective brake
        to keep from colliding
stanzas askew
        the chrome   bump   er
before   us

        and for the next ten kilometres
i ask tired bus driver eyes in the mirror

we'll never arrive will we?
no son, never again.

3.
rush hour could be a space where you open

forget the time
you'll get there when you get there
try   to enjoy the peace of
a quiet ride by the window
rustling paper   muffled cough

all control is with our driver
            and the gods of traffic and highway capacity
this space might   be the best you've ever known
                        imagine that
as long as you   don't want
more for the shoulder
        for the leg   for your huge
                        growing body
        stretched   on a twenty mile bed
by a river   under old stars

The Silver Sky

for Allan Briesmaster

The sign girl flips *Stop* and *Slow*
    like disappearing coins,
    sleight of hand on a stick

We crawl along the raised expressway,
gaze through tinted bus windows
at the work crew
replacing steel rods twisted, rusty,
exhumed from thirty years of concrete,
shadowed tufts of grass below

Their hard hats, jeans and faces are covered
with the dust of a billion commuters,
from cars that went through guard rails, behind tow trucks,
hosted heart attacks, lost licences,
tracked all the vanished hours on dashboard clocks
that tick in junkyards to this day

In the distance, the inscrutable city –
silver rectangles and pyramids clean
as the gleaming coffee truck and
these fresh steel rods which,
placed end to end, would pierce
the overcast sky, touch the waves
of cloud, a sea above
of empty silver where no bird
(or fish) flies

No longer roused from sleep
my brain leaves no dreams on my doorstep
but under the escarpment unwritten poems
gather at dusk, make impatient shadow sounds
a hunting owl swerves in silence.

Click on OK
(after Ferlinghetti)

Let's go
let's escape the virtual this and that
take our big slap in the face while we still can.
Don't wait for the systems administrator
his parameters, his default.
Don't fax forward your virtual signature for
virtual cash. Your account has been cleaned out
by network accounting.
Don't query or execute any more.
Click on OK.

Let's go
this too too solid central processor
is for earning, not learning.
Let go of your user profile
it weighs nothing after all.
You are the shrinking pupil of history.
Stop bathing in the light of your desktop.
Subvert it back into the candle
we used ages ago, for reading and writing after dark.
Pull the plug.
If you feel drained
Click on OK.

Let's go
far north beyond the electrical line
as the last of an endangered species
to be saved at the brink. Or not.
Forget procedures. Forget
how to log on and exit.

Is someone watching? Monitoring?
That's an audience, God perhaps.
Pirouette before you go.
Be the spider on the underside
of all this.
Slide through the crack in that window.
Click on OK.

User Instructions

Gather up the Windows menus with both hands
Double-click the *Mary, Mother of Jesus* icon
Interrogate the spreadsheet for the bottom line
Discover a mistake and cherish it
don't sue the company
or worry about the unpaid hydro account

Accelerate across the screen until your cursor is squealing
and you are hemmed in by error messages
Approach the three terrorists crucified outside Jerusalem
Use the Control Panel to change the colour of their suffering
Keep looking inward, for just the right tone of blue

Clean your monitor and power supply
Here's useful information: Working ...
Do you smell dinner burning?

Take out the garbage
Run to the store, trudge home loaded
Stare at the receding back of your father who understands
he will die, that you will die

You haven't had a good night's sleep in years
Activate a screen saver
Watch the string sculpture bounce
Your power's dropping, twisting
Before the bathwater freezes over
jump in
grab this live wire with both hands

Insomnia

silence   then
          a dog barks at the dog home world
glistening in the night sky
          the streets echo with hot rods
sometimes the cops chase, sometimes they wait

I must give up believing
          your Picasso coffee table book
will render the burning vitality of paint
          that Bruckner's dialogue with God
can be heard one movement at a time
I must give up worrying
          the back door is being jimmied
                    or set on fire
                              while I wait for morning

this dark living room magnifies the drone
          of one mosquito
and the thump of neighbours who don't know
          that two a.m. has been designated
as sleepy time
          by the Geneva convention
that ironing board draped with shirts
is just another detail to prevent
hearing the far-off piano run of imagination

like cold sprinklers on hot skin, something sharp
in this couch
          reminds me
          of your new mysterious painting
hung on the opposite wall
waiting for sunrise

Sleep

trying too hard, my body jerks
is this the right bed?
height of pillow
              pyjamas, gown
or naked?
                     turn off the street lights!

when it finds the right position
it pops like a lock
        and releases its version of the day
        from a dark place where claws are tucked tight
        and wings hover, straining to stay in air

i can't tell you what happens next
but when i wake on my back
my fist has penetrated the world
my tongue has licked the animals of
its own kind, my feet have run
riot in sneakers through fashion houses
i have been Plastic Man, stretching to save
toddlers on balconies, cats in trees

rayonized and cotton covered, bound in ropes
and bounced on tendons
i have escaped into the surfer's curl at
Malibu, worn a tuxedo
to the senior prom, married many
and divorced a few, crashed a car
and laughed
that's my body's idea of a life
it also mourns

what it cannot have
i gave it a lover
        but it's vain and demands more

it dreams of revenge, of pruning roses
the prick, the blood released
through the heavy clay of the torso
it puts fingers in shit, in my mouth

i wake
on sweated sheets, moments after my
head went down
i am clean, like
an empty plate ready to accept food
in the morning

Worry

At 5 a.m. the city barely moves
I'm whispering at yesterday's voices
    keep it down, leave me alone

In pursuit of stillness
the old Chinese do tai-chi on the soccer field,
their bodies look like an alphabet,
an ensemble prayer I would wish
after a lifetime of trying to give language
the slip

Oh worry, yes
a childish panic mired in logic,
my neighbour's accordion churns in the wall
I pray his racket will
strangle him by the chorus, his scales bouncing like
flaccid springs from lifeless hands
Dear Lord, please expunge my depression,
these thoughts of murder,
such hysterical statements

His footfalls descend the apartment stairs
I slow to a quiet hum,
cursed with a tick tock relentlessness
when what I want is a beatific blank,
the calm to stare down at the city
from the twenty-third floor
without the feeling of *jump*

To live in the silence after
the last note of a massive symphony,
to be the playful nothing made up
of thousands holding their breath
without applause

Go to work, hands
unpack your instruments,
your conductor's drinking in a bar
write it all down
don't leave a note in my mind.

Ice Overhead

The eavestrough is down
twisted and split, like an arm
torn off the house

The contractor shuffles
words about
how these months of melt and freeze
melted and froze
and subtly built a battleship of ice in the eaves
high where he worked last summer
and how long that whitish hull must have hovered
waiting for critical mass
                (he's not really so poetic ...)

Last night came the roaring drop
that tore through the aluminum order
of sluices on an old house
                an aqueduct for the proud owners' money

It launched without champagne
the last roof ice of winter
created for a man and wife
who could not stand back and look up
who kept the windows closed
who kept their solitude and angry voices down

Squinting up into the sun
I see how sharp and sudden the air
our fallen pieces
of inertia

Layoff Rumours

The new president's memo is blunt
Changing the direction of this organization
will be like turning the Queen Mary.
Iceberg metaphors drift through our office.

Some passengers are to be thrown into the North Atlantic
insufficient life jackets
none trained to lower a boat
set the oars.
Seniority crouches in a cabin
going down with the ship.

Some will drown unemployed
rather than bob to the surface
screaming for help.
Some will turn over and over with
fear this is the end of everything.
Some want a new thing
for the rest of their lives
won't huddle in the ballroom
the chandelier tilting sixty degrees
as the furniture and cutlery crash to one wall.

We wish for the discipline of a navy
but have been out of uniform too long.
Our resumes go fluttering astern like gulls
spreading over millions
of whitecaps to the horizon.

If Accountants Were Cowboys

the cowpoke knocks on the president's door
tentative after hard-riding the dusty audit trail
a cross-country round-up, night and day there's still
an outstanding balance in his saddle bags –
a corral transaction history report,
predicted prices at next week's credit cattle auction,
a sales prospectus from the fence menders

he sips from his water bag, prepares to sing the cowboy
song of unrequited deficit financing,
grins to think of how they're gonna force that rustler
into bankruptcy, for once and for all
push his carcass out for the buzzards
and the rattlesnakes
on the plains of litigation.

Frank Is My Shepherd

I shall not want.
He leadeth me to green pastures
and 23% annual returns.
He leadeth me beside still waters.
He restoreth my soul
and my profits from the overseas markets.
He leadeth me in the path of monthly purchases,
for his funds' sake.

Even though I walk through the shadow
of a major correction,
I fear no drop,
for thou art with me.
Thy statements and thy staff,
they comfort me.

Thou preparest a table before me,
despite the comments of the Federal Reserve.
In the presence of mine enemies,
thou anointest my head with oil.
When the energy sector overflows,
surely dividends and write-offs shall follow me
all the days of my life,
and I shall obsess over my investments forever.

Tremors

During an earthquake
buildings seem to fall inward.
Demolition experts know the splendour
of collapsing a skyscraper just so.

Your brother's wife calls
to say he didn't
come home again last night.
It's a family act
what they have done these months
to hide the stress
how children, aunts, and uncles must
play their parts.
We sit at home and
when the telephone rings
another crack opens in the floor.

Their marriage now a white dwarf star
an image of happiness sent light years ago
to burn in memory.

Shut the photo albums
with news of how things were, or who we are.
Clouds now block all star-gazing.
We return home, gently glare
at the phone in the hall
          when suddenly the handset falls, then bricks and walls
and last – amid clay chips and scattered books –
one
pot lid drops
from the sky.

The Last Ride

The air conditioned bus
hisses him into a dream of early fall
of ripe peaches and pears
and rutting with the girls in the office

This morning he forgets he has been paid to resign
and suddenly the limitless future
feeds an anger, sets him smirking through the world
behind blue-tint glasses of rage
and a new dream of shooting
the director of Employee Assistance

Bus slows for traffic and he falls into
calm consideration
of his years
accomplishments and promotions
marks of his corporate motility
but also the wrinkling of his crazy days
and unchased young ambition

Road turns bumpy past the lake
jars his jaw on the window glass
soon enough, the last traffic jam
    Friday passage to a weekend
    without end

Passing

Sculpted words about
furnace checks and investments
                swirl
through the phone and up the chimney
money gasps out bargains with every mailing

He is immune
in his dream of a young man
                who hurled stones
extended his body, his arm going with the arc
                of the gritty thing thrown again and again
until plop in the waves
                                of the giant green blue Ontario

On cold afternoons
he hurdled the cinder track
toppled aluminum stands with an omnipotent
trailing leg
won a child's trophy

Lately the race has been without end
                and though he gets quarterly statements
                of his success
after many years in the office
                his hips ache
his brother has run away
                to join the information circus
                to develop a loyalty program for the perfect
                unknown customer

His pets were bored and escaped
        into the street where they reverted
        to weeds and butterflies
his wife speaks
banners of letters move sideways
        and disappear, his eye no longer follows
his friends can't hold on
                they scoop him up again and again
into the office chair   the body slides down
                                        the chair rolls away

Joe

one life was enough
but the blue world opened and allowed him,
like an astronaut, back into orbit

We thought our neighbour Joe
was dead, but there he was
one July morning.
In his wheelchair, on the porch
in pure white running shoes with velcro tabs.

His clasped hands,
his narrow lips said
he felt fine for ninety.
He could no longer walk,
but where would he go?

So at ease to be out of the hospital
once again in his own home
with his sixty-year old son to mother him.
They both wore Bermuda shorts and Panama hats,
easy shade against the bright sun and his son's concern
for Joe's gossamer skin.
And his face,
where not even the smallest ambition
rippled his smile –
a man returned to heaven
in the summer breeze

Echoes of Wilderness

We need to let animals loose in our houses,
the wolf to escape with a pan in his teeth,
and streams of animals toward the horizon
racing with something silent in each mouth.

       – *Outside*
           William Stafford

To Touch a Bird

The beak is guardian and brain of the bird.
You must pass it to reach
the heart,
that essential wildness you want.

Do not show your fear of bites
by wearing gloves
or a smile.

The bird speaks with its eye and tail,
builds a nest among the smokestacks,
steals sandwich bread from the men in the hot mill.
You want to escape?
Keep your hands in your pockets,
place your cheek on the bird's back.
Even when closed, how broad the wings!

Understand,
when they choose
you are mated for life.

Variation on Colville's *Hound in Field*

The young hound floats
one paw visible
muscular in midturn
attends his own nose
bullet black over the snow
body about to follow
to change entirely
as if he has just caught
the acrid truth
about some squirrel
fox, another dog beyond the frame.

Deep orange eye, black lid
that knows and wants
to see a darting rabbit or bird,
his sloping ears will miss
no footfall, no rising wing.

Even if
after I walk away the prey bolts through
the background into the forest
there will still be
the dark curtain before which
the chase begins
the turn before which
the supreme hound glistens
frozen
while he pours out
his fur-charged leaping life.

For the Mosquito

From still water
and cedar hedgerows, you find
      your way into the mouths
      of purple martins and swallows.
A few of you splatter on my windshield.

Many more softly fizz
past sleepy ears
wings whirring you to a fine blur.
My mammal meat hands are up, attempt
the one-hand catch or bruising splat
while five other needles I cannot see
suspend over blood targets.

My unease when I wake
is by dinner time aflame
with itch itch itch itch
up sleeves and trouser legs.
My hosts stare: *Keep the damn door closed kids!*

A three-week life seems short,
but you are three thousand species,
we, the occupying army on earth.
You can take three times your weight in blood
to make eggs, you can wait
for the icecaps to melt, the plains to submerge
for the whiff of some new
dinosaur
to taste.

The Fin Whale at Cheticamp

There were no life jackets on the lobster boat
our pilot took into the sway blue-green
that curled to the horizon. Every moment
hope rose and was dashed against the hull.
Eyes were tricked, and again were tricked,
give up, give out, give over the sea said,
while cormorants gathered above the crests
looking for the white blow stream.

We, so noisy and slow in the glinting cold
where waves might be the tails of whales.

Then –
close enough to surprise even our pilot –
we saw the fin so small for the seventy tons
coming directly at the port side of the bow.
He could have flipped us
or split us with one short smash of snout.

But he dived instead, sank his power
to its salty zenith
and surfaced many yards off,
blow spout showering.
He knew us to be fragile wood and glass bobbing
in the Gulf of St. Lawrence so cold and he so huge and warm,
his shadow a black, inert spot, interrupting the ocean.

We were calmed, inspected
and he – holding no grudge for those thousands of hunts
which had ended with thrashing blood-red water –
saw our cameras, how we needed

to see him
to be vulnerable, ever-bobbing
to watch one trick,
like a back flop or dive, tail perpendicular,
to discover
we had been enriched by his mercy.

Parrot Breeding Season

1.

Amazon Stanley lumbers down the perch
snaps at the treat I have placed there
seizes and crushes and grinds
a stick from his toy basket
flings it to the floor
a warning to my fingers
he's chomped pieces
from a table leg, frayed a speaker cable

He needs a cavity in which
to raise his young
      – always in a tree –
this wooden house sustains us all
but cannot accommodate
such furious tidal craving
I shoo him with a blanket, he waddles away
groans at the length of spring days
at autumn leaves on wallpaper
in his secret heart
time tightens

2.

Olivia looks at the chicken egg in the sink
bound for the compost heap outdoors
a hard-boiled oversight that never
made egg salad sandwich
dinner or midnight snack

Olivia, proud of her plumage
tilts her head, one eye upon
the pebbled white shell
listens, thinks incubation
waits for it to cheep
and betray its cold promise

Never mated, she remembers the nest
Never on a farm, she knows the hen

Trying to Mother

Birds outdoors
settle one by one on the feeder
taunt squirrels   watch the cat
Somewhere in the bush
a hen lays an egg every two days
After six she settles down to warm them
seems not to grieve if an egg fails
She knows the inscrutable face of nature
and her faithful mate

Indoors we have baby budgies in a nest box
An accident has killed our hen
In five days we've kept half
the clutch alive
incubation no substitute
for a few feathered ounces
sitting and warming
Her mate seems not to hear the babies' hungry
sheep-cheep-chirk
He has no knowledge
is not a griever
will let them die

Our hen would observe
her chicks' eyes under transparent lids
gently tap the tiny point of a baby's beak
which would have instantly opened
to receive her sharp stream of life

I poise with a syringe
of thickening brown gruel
poke a featherless face with the plastic tip
my hands too much for tiny weightless birds
They are pink souls
not fleshy enough for a cat to bother
Some mouths open, some do not

A ghost flits in
and out of the kitchen
demands I not fail
      stick it out warm feed warm feed
Try them try to try to
try to raise those that keep cheeping

A chick two days old when its mother died
has died too, a transparent sac of organs
and the last egg – which we thought void
and had left in the box to preserve warmth –
hatched itself in the morning
and died in the evening
All day I tinker a heating pad around
the nest box

I am no engineer, no hen
though when I catch myself crying
at the table
I realize I might have been

Lines Written after Watching a Huge Truck of Chickens Pass on the 401

The tiny orange crates packed fifteen high
are roped and hooked to the flatbed. In each,
a living puff of animal husbandry
brain, beak, claws   flightlessness.

The truck roars, the wind whips through the crates,
mud flaps swing hard and every second
a few white feathers fly up   up
over
the highway.
My eyes tangle in blue sky, white clouds.

They are going to die today and if these birds
are frightened you cannot tell.
Are they thinking of the barn, the pen, the feed?
Tires around us whine, motors harmonize
high and low, air brakes and clutches groan
like shattering breath.

They have to know, and so
release puffs of white into the playful slipstream,
vestiges of self, of egg and yard
of sunlight and rain.
Bodies pressed tight in the supply chain,
hi-ho, hi-ho, it's off we go, to be efficiently chopped
and plucked, seasoned, packaged
and popped into mammalian jaws at $5.99 a pound.

When I catch up, they're stopped in traffic.
I see a head poke through a broken orange bar.

Instinctively she rears back, raises her wings, stabs,
and another bar gives way into bright day
over this black road.

The policeman's having morning coffee while he runs a radar trap.
Traffic eases, then tears off fast enough for a ticket.
We're all in a rush today, officer, all making good time
or late for appointments, as the case may be,
like a flatbed of chickens.

Bird Watching

City pigeons have noted
the falcon nest on the building ledge,
have gone suburban
but must compete with the Canada geese for the routes.

Honk out of sky –
the sharp original
for which no amount of solitude or eastern religion
can prepare the ear.
Back with my head,
up my eyes
the flying V of revelation says,
profoundly,
Bye.

The lead goose scolds three stragglers
off the left wing, cares not for their effort
only for keeping shape
in the air, an expensively open medium
with death downwind.

A few geese nest in the parking lot, in the landscaper's
rock garden. Hen ignores the come and go
of dump trucks and jumbo jets –
with a clenched heart, she sits and every other day
stretches wide to lay
the warm drop of a new bird, rotates her eggs
with her beak, webbed feet tucked like ground cover
under her babies' shells.
Courage makes her neck straight,
her eye opens silence, hypnotizes me
while her mate sneaks up to attack this poem.

osprey shadows overhead
snaking soft sliver of dreaming river

4.

ghosts and their descendants crowd the interpretive centre
at Frank, Alberta where ten times a day
the avalanche replays
the miners' folly
death by technology
revelations in geology

5.

the helicopter carries a bear in a net
drugged and bound for a distant range because a teenager
offered it an ice cream cone
the video includes an elder native's voiceover:
The spirit of the bear has left this land
            the bear knew well enough to bite the hand
that fed it
and make its getaway

6.

binoculars are no use
below the peak of Whistler Mountain
thousands of heavy shoes crunch
the path and scramble to stay within the curbs
to not step on fragile flowers
or the alpine meadow
which is snow covered, foot printed

everyone turns for the rain shrouded
view of Jasper
            and ahead, the diverging paths
            of silence, disappearance

Consumers

Money has no memory.

The car *consumes* gas
and the thesaurus gives us
exhaust, waste, drain, dissipate, fritter away
the last bird in the jungle will exhaust
its heart pounding for its mate
among the logs on the river

We'll find that bird, save it if we have to
        even deal with the *non-consuming*
        which is unknown
we'll sell vacations to the place with no name
not enough fish for the business plan
        a few of those rare apes maybe
show me the zoo concept
        this is an emerging market
tiger: great concept, looks cool
but won't domesticate,
no petting, no initial public offering

Let's jump on that theme park idea
produce a CD-ROM for the schools
trade our right to pollute for their
right to consume
it's important to make jobs for the locals
get this economy up to speed
hey look, parrots in the eaves of
those new suburban houses
get me an artist
get me some of that local colour

Muskoka Blues
for R. W. Megens

We drive north
as secret agents, as hostages
slow sweating every minute
along a trail of red tail lights at sunset.
After dark, high beams blaze
through the rear view mirror
their double-barrelled farewell.

We arrive as strange
dinner guests entrusted with knives,
onions, and fresh meat.
Fingers on the cutting board,
I'm ready to eat your great unknown
animals, your spices, and wash everything down
with soft whisky talk all night around
a baby in a swing.

At dawn outside the tempered window
wild daffodils fire shots of yellow through the trees;
like a city dog, I crash yapping
to the water's edge.
My heart slides,
my foot green-algae-slips into the bay
away from concepts like cottages
and ownership of graves. This silence rings.

Last night my sleep streamed through the window
as moonlight to the forest edge. Then crows at dawn awoke
and squawked and stabbed and looked
and stabbed on that hill,
the perfect place to fall and be buried.

Samizdat

Much of what is said here
must be said twice,
a reminder that no one
takes an immediate interest in the pain of others.

– *The Blues*
        Billy Collins

Logos

Adam got credit for naming the animals
　　　but the animals are history
said Logos, his third son.
　　　They're too selfish.
　　　See my gifts:
units of measurement and maps.

And with these guides
Logos decremented pints of blood from hearts,
　　　turned flesh into kilos and foot-longs,
replaced the forests with property values,
created statistical performance,
radiation levels, pollen counts,
productivity per shift,
thresholds of pain for study at police academies.
He counted Adam's animals in the pig barn.

As Logos grew into a labour management system,
he optimized the hours and the sick days,
found others to work for him. He has solved
our hungers but will not cease
counting to the largest, the highest.

He will never dismiss us.
Only dementia really bothers him,
so here on the page I will drool,
bite my fingers 'til they bleed.
Spread this poem as samizdat,
chant it from my cell,
and just to spite you Logos,
I will record every breathing thing I see
and describe them goddamn
breathlessly.

Improvisation on a Hot Autumn Day

Untied strands of poetry thwap
against my glasses. The romantic television car
hides its engineering,
its struggle with mountain inclines.
And once I've found a pen, I find
all I'm producing
      are present participles,
weighted words
      none that *Leap! Good boy!*
while I stand in the shackles
of this graph paper
like a mathematician.

Whereas migrants from other tongues
want *here,* the nuanced sound to calm their ears,
we, richly resident, crave *there,*
to slip away, think *road,* not *knot*
the necktie that defines
the chance to stay put and prosper.

A store sign wishes me a *Happy Hallowe'en*
and all I think is contradiction. A girl with a voice
like a pair of scissors goes *Yup*
at the door of a fabric shop.
I pause under eavestrough to eavesdrop
to catch cutting words
as they squirt through seams in the crowd.
Voices rush and block the flow,
      conversation
           language   Crash.

Through schoolyard and churchyard
and double-rut alleys I walk.
Through golden leaves of maple trees
the sun runs warm fingers down my back,
leaves sweat rivulets on my bark body.
Steel rails sidle and weave through
this graph grid of streets and yards,
blow a trainless whistle up to the main line.

I want to hear
the streak of juggled
language be-bop stroked and strutting,
          to forget
to wait for some reply,
to chase ghosts, dance past the tracks
of melody, wary of the unutterable
which might be
lurking in the shower when I get home.

Poetry at the Jaffé Lounge

beat   bold
       black blouse   slacks
       folding   unfolding arms

the young poets
squiggle out their bios for the hostess

this smoky room gets warm
gets nerves up and down before their time
to read

clean-cut   at a lone table
a boy holds his chin gently between thumb and forefinger
squints at the paintings
the ceiling drapes, the track lighting
and the slim lounge owner behind the bar
is he cool?
       am i sophisticated?

the room has ears for all:
      black draped waif
          body builder in a leather jacket
a rasta kid who wows them   with positive vibration

they pull out
      not truth exactly
but words that get a laugh
      tales of bedbugs and laundry in Greece:
personal dramas
that overlook the Parthenon, the Muses
      Odysseus

the hostess flips her hair
reads from some magazines
          calls that poetry too
in the corner   a girl holds her boy
her fingers give him courage to let go
                    in a moment

to rise and read something that inspires
the old guy at the bar
who fondly remembers
first drafts
the earnest talk of other poets
                    praise
the power of young lines

In the Bigger Bookstores

The computer issues
a synthesizer fanfare,
there's software loading!
The children shriek.

The achievement of the correct store environment depends on
builders and staff carefully following corporate procedures for
wood panelling, shelves, merchandise, stuffed armchairs, and
aisles.

By the faux fireplace,
    a rumpled man reads aloud.
His gestures draw no listener near,
    he's written lightning to the page,
        dangerous in close quarters, here
        so much flammable paper.
Instead he moves gingerly among the metaphors,
    holds up his gems, dances alone
        soft and lightly blue.
He brakes
to a grumbling, earthquaking notion,
        sudden nimble verbs begin to jump
    his poem's final octane go.
He calls, sings into
    a soft and rapid end
    whispered words of rose
        soft breasts of temptation.

While the policy states that public readings are to be encouraged
if the author can draw a crowd, customers who would otherwise
be in the store are not to be disturbed. The microphone is to be shut
off in favour of the Muzak.®

Hard pine floors are thus kept clear
of grown men fainting
though not of babies wailing
nor empty cups of cappuccino
discarded by the washroom door.

Tasnim Sings

Tasnim sings so softly
I barely hear the sound of her Indian childhood

Her calculator totals mortgage tax not paid
Money, the phone bleats
men and tailored women rush about
voices shout over throttling neckties
      Give me that in writing

Tasnim sings of a small village
of a sari and elephants on the logging road
while overhead yellow and green parrots
flash like anachronisms
In the cities of the north wealth must accumulate
Tasnim cannot share with anyone but
her employer and tax officials
the sum of her work
which in harness with millions of others
has owned and taken over a million villages, parrots, elephants

Tasnim sings so softly
she is no longer heard
beneath the bellow of vice-presidents
who are just helping out
an angry red sun on the horizon

Reverse Shoplifting

He parks far from the monolith,
seeks no staff, goes softly
on the hardwood floor
with three copies of his poetry book
in each coat pocket.
Slips one into *Bargains*, where lately he's found
the greater poets he admires.

Continues through *Literature, History, Humour* –
grim serious about this business
of product placement.
Palms his book onto shelves
where the weight of everything known
laps against the dam of store security.
Sleepy management eyes ripple
dreams of golf and retirement parties.
This retail renegade stops only to flirt with
the young cashier.

He leaves empty-handed. Day by day,
he paddles up-river
through the front door, up the wide aisles,
giving himself away, undiscovered.

At last he glides a copy across the counter.
She smiles at his wordless eyes,
forgets her aches, slips off her shoes,
picks up his offering.
He wants to autograph her hand,
displays of paper pyramids begin falling
in the breeze, before the wall.
He pricks her heart to release
a storm of new poems that flood
the mall and parking lot.

Variation on Beethoven's Violin Concerto

1. Allegro ma non troppo

breathe slow   breathe deep
adjust that hair pin   better
force out the air
don't gulp it back in

am I relaxed yet?
          violin what about you?
wipe strings
fingers curl and straighten
instrument under chin
          how did anyone ever play without Louis Spohr's chin rest?

just once I would like to make this walk
from the backstage to light
without nerves
one nerve four strings tuned   in control
curtain back yes
ow hard spotlight don't squint
relax
the face
                    the wrist
think limp

heads in rows flinch uncomfortably in evening dress
          here goes my titchy stage smile

years ago Mrs. Weigand said
*Vanity and ego are required for the profession. Stand on the stage because
you have earned the right to be there. No one moves you. The audience,
conductor, orchestra, the hall, the seats, the drapes, the nails which hold
the stage together. You own them all.*

sweep arm raise bow tantalise
what do they expect?
fireworks, sex, languid
contemplation, sleep? what am I thinking?
check tuning of the A string
old conductor whispers in my ear for luck
flirts with me for their amusement

he looks like a tortoise bent back leathery face and bald dome
rehearsal was hard but occasionally
a sweet mingling
a workout
attend

audience breathes as one
silence strikes a slow tympani
slow   slow   my   heart
keep time
breathe that first note   a pure soft o
a ring of smoke   that
            floats
            above
gone
into the past

somewhere at the back of the hall
            a black hole is consuming
            each bar each page
music may be stretched but not retained
            or regained
the only sounds
            are those to come
I only have
to make them perfect
as perfect

more perfect
keep perfect

oh it's impossible   try to dance
            without using your body
        try to not be seduced
            by this piece you have loved forever
such distance of time and space
                and sound
        he couldn't hear

        no
        black tortoise don't turn so soon
                                    orchestra slowing

        come come come come rise
        come come come come rise

is my one Guarneri the leader here?
am I the guiding   the call?

        song song song song prayer
        draw   me   pull   us   there

thirty other strings   all on the baton
                                homogenous slow
        I must watch   for my chance
        with this tortoise
                    to change his tempo

        he he he he them
        he-them   he and they must listen to me
        and follow
        imagine the arthritic hand
        running out of time
        splashing notes on the page

Mrs. Weigand always saying *Even Larghetto requires some tension.*
Don't wallow in the Romantic vista. Give strength, muscle.

whose tears am I raising? his jaw his cheek his lips
        his fine young body tonight after dinner
he's in my mind forever
now use the thought of him
to
move

use these

three
bold
stokes

to

3. Rondo

      come horns
      come winds
      we dance and run with measure that springs
      that tortoise and I
      agree at last
              is right

      here's the melody coming back
      we walk and wander
      wend and amble
      but I'm riding now
      as if the eddies of air
      were charging horses
                    under my hand
      lifting us all

watch it strings
keep close through these runs
no slipping now

I'll pull down the tree
till it bends to me
my bow over your plodding
baton
tortoise will slow
but I will lead
I must go
go
give them a melody to carry whistling to the night
trill and pause
keep waiting for it
                    now go

up and down
off and around
I sing at last
the iron and silk
the river and flow
that light on water
the black hole filling
sated with sound
a thousand arrows
on the air
and yes
there's more
the tightness gone
we can win have won
a hundred notes
the rich sweet chord
and there and pause
and there, motif

and there and pause
and there, motif
and there
and there
and there
and there

breathe

Acknowledgements

Thanks to Allan Briesmaster, A.F. Moritz, Jim Slominski, Mary Ellen Csamer, and Donna Langevin for their careful reading and valuable comments on the manuscript. Many individual poems were improved by the insights of members of the *new writing workshop* in Hamilton.

Special thanks to Maureen Whyte for her vision and dedication to poetry. Also I'm very grateful to Janice Jackson and Bernard Kelly for providing such a powerful cover.

Selected poems were previously published in *Journal of the Writing Space, New Quarterly, Lichen, Kairos, Between a Dock and a High Place,* and *Dreamcatcher.* Many thanks to the editors of those journals. Additionally, four poems here are reprinted from my first collection because they seemed to fit the thematic concerns of this book. These are reprinted with permission of the Jasper Press.

This book is for Vera and John Pannell.

About the Author

In 1996, the Jasper Press published Chris Pannell's first solo collection of poetry, three broadsheets entitled *Fractures, Subluxations and Dislocations*. This set subsequently won the Hamilton & Region Arts Council poetry book award. In 1999, his first full-length book, entitled *Sorry I Spent Your Poem*, was published by watershedBooks. Since 1993 he has led the *new writing workshop* at Hamilton Artists Inc. He edited both anthologies the group has produced: *Your Baggage is in Buffalo* (1994) and *Between a Dock and a High Place* (1997). His non-fiction has appeared in *The Globe and Mail* and in various computer industry journals. He lives in Hamilton, Ontario.